Delicious croissant canapes

Irresistible Croissant Canapés

While every precaution has been taken in the preparation of this book, the publisher assumes no responsibility for errors or omissions, or for damages resulting from the use of the information contained herein.

DELICIOUS CROISSANT CANAPES

First edition. December 13, 2023.

Copyright © 2023 Jose Maria.

ISBN: 979-8223996484

Written by Jose Maria.

Table of Contents

Jose Maria

I. Introduction

A. Brief Overview of Croissant Canapés

Croissant canapés are a delightful fusion of the classic French croissant and elegant finger foods. These miniature treats offer a perfect balance of flaky, buttery goodness and a variety of flavorful toppings. From savory to sweet, croissant canapés elevate the art of entertaining, providing a versatile canvas for culinary creativity.

B. Importance of Presentation and Flavor Combination

The allure of croissant canapés lies not only in their taste but also in their presentation. These bite-sized wonders add a touch of sophistication to any gathering, making them ideal for brunches, parties, and special occasions. The combination of textures – the crisp flakiness of the croissant paired with rich fillings – creates a culinary experience that is both indulgent and memorable.

Mastering the art of flavor combination is key to crafting the perfect croissant canapé. The delicate balance of savory and sweet, paired with complementary textures, ensures each bite is a harmonious symphony of tastes. The right pairing can transform a simple croissant into a culinary masterpiece, leaving a lasting impression on your guests.

C. Tips for Working with Croissants

Working with croissants requires a gentle touch to preserve their delicate layers and ensure a perfect outcome. Here are some essential tips:

Selecting the Perfect Croissants:

- Choose high-quality croissants, whether store-bought or homemade. Look for a golden-brown color, indicating proper baking.

Proper Slicing and Shaping:

- When slicing croissants for canapés, use a sharp knife to maintain their flaky layers. Aim for uniformity in size for a polished presentation.

Baking Tips for Flaky Perfection:

- If baking croissants at home, follow precise baking instructions to achieve a golden, flaky exterior and a soft, buttery interior.

Storing and Reheating Croissants:

- Store croissants in an airtight container to preserve freshness. When reheating, use an oven or toaster oven for a few minutes to regain their crisp texture.

Embrace the art of working with croissants, and you'll unlock the potential to create stunning canapés that captivate both the eyes and the palate.

II. Chapter 1: Essential Croissant Canapé Techniques

A. Selecting the Perfect Croissants

Choosing the ideal croissants is a crucial first step in crafting exceptional canapés. Dive deeper into the selection process:

Freshness is Key:

- Seek out croissants that are as fresh as possible. If buying from a bakery, aim for those baked on the same day. For store-bought options, check for the freshest expiration or production date.

Golden-Brown Exterior:

- Examine the color of the croissants. A uniform golden-brown exterior indicates thorough baking. It suggests that the dough has risen appropriately, leading to a crisp crust and a soft, flaky interior.

Butter Content:

- Turn your attention to the ingredient list. A higher butter content is a positive sign, contributing to the richness and flavor of the croissants. Look for those made with real butter for an authentic taste.

B. Proper Slicing and Shaping

Precision in slicing and shaping enhances the visual appeal and texture of your croissant canapés:

Use a Sharp, Serrated Knife:

- Employ a sharp, serrated knife to ensure clean cuts. The serrated edge helps cut through the delicate layers without compressing them, preserving the croissant's flaky texture.

Horizontal Slicing:

- Adopt a horizontal slicing technique for canapés. This method provides a broad, stable base for toppings, allowing for easy assembly and a consistent bite-size experience.

Consistent Shaping:

- Strive for uniformity in the shape and size of each sliced croissant. Consistency ensures that each canapé is not only visually appealing but also delivers a balanced combination of flavors in every bite.

C. Baking Tips for Flaky Perfection

Whether baking from scratch or reheating, follow detailed tips to achieve the desired flaky perfection:

Follow Baking Instructions:

- When baking from scratch, meticulously follow the recipe instructions. Pay attention to details such as dough resting times, oven temperature, and baking duration. These factors contribute to the development of flaky layers.

Preheat the Oven Thoroughly:

- Ensure the oven is fully preheated before placing the croissants inside. A hot oven kickstarts the leavening process, resulting in a rise and the development of those sought-after flaky layers.

Rotate During Baking:

- If baking multiple croissants on a sheet, consider rotating the pan halfway through the baking time. This promotes even exposure to heat, preventing uneven browning and ensuring a consistent texture.

D. Storing and Reheating Croissants

Preserve the freshness and texture of croissants with thoughtful storage and reheating practices:

Airtight Storage:

- After initial use, store any remaining croissants in an airtight container or a sealed plastic bag. This prevents exposure to air and helps maintain their moisture, preventing them from becoming dry.

Reheating in the Oven:

- Opt for the oven or toaster oven when reheating croissants. Preheat to 350°F (175°C) and warm for 5-7 minutes. This method effectively restores the crisp exterior and soft interior, closely replicating the freshly baked experience.

Avoid Microwave Usage:

- Refrain from using the microwave for reheating, as it tends to compromise the flaky texture of the croissants. The oven method ensures a more consistent result.

By paying meticulous attention to these nuanced details in the selection, slicing, baking, and storage of croissants, you set the stage for creating canapés that embody the epitome of flaky perfection.

III. Chapter 2: Classic Croissant Canapé Recipes

A. Smoked Salmon and Cream Cheese Delight

Ingredients:

- 6 croissants (freshly baked or store-bought)
- 150g smoked salmon, thinly sliced
- 150g cream cheese, softened
- 1 tablespoon fresh dill, chopped
- 1 tablespoon capers, drained
- 1 lemon, thinly sliced
- Freshly ground black pepper, to taste

Instructions:
Prepare the Croissants:

- If using store-bought croissants, follow the instructions for baking.
- For homemade croissants, ensure they are fully baked and have a golden-brown color.

Slice and Spread:

- Allow the croissants to cool slightly before horizontally slicing them.
- Spread a generous layer of softened cream cheese on the bottom half of each croissant.

Layer with Smoked Salmon:

- Place a few slices of smoked salmon on top of the cream cheese.

Garnish:

- Sprinkle chopped fresh dill and capers over the smoked salmon.
- Add a couple of thin lemon slices on top.

Assemble and Serve:

- Place the top half of the croissants on the assembled bottoms, creating sandwich-like canapés.
- Arrange on a platter and serve immediately for a burst of flavor in every bite.

B. Brie and Fig Jam Elegance

Ingredients:

- 6 croissants (freshly baked or store-bought)
- 200g Brie cheese, sliced
- 1/2 cup fig jam
- 1/4 cup chopped walnuts (optional)
- Fresh thyme leaves for garnish
-

Instructions:
Prepare the Croissants:

- If using store-bought croissants, bake according to the package instructions.
- For homemade croissants, ensure they are fully baked with a golden-brown hue.

Slice and Layer:

- Allow croissants to cool slightly before slicing horizontally.
- Lay slices of Brie on the bottom halves of the croissants

Spread Fig Jam:

- Generously spread fig jam over the Brie slices.

Optional Crunch:

- For added texture, sprinkle chopped walnuts over the fig jam.

Assemble and Garnish:

- Place the top halves of the croissants on the assembled bottoms, creating elegant canapés.
- Garnish with fresh thyme leaves for a touch of sophistication.

Serve Fresh:

- Arrange on a platter and serve immediately to enjoy the harmonious blend of Brie and fig flavors.

Continue with the remaining classic croissant canapé recipes, or let me know if you'd like details on any specific one!

C. Prosciutto and Arugula Bliss

Ingredients:

- 6 croissants (freshly baked or store-bought)
- 100g prosciutto, thinly sliced
- 1 cup fresh arugula
- 1/4 cup balsamic glaze
- Freshly ground black pepper, to taste

Instructions:

Prepare the Croissants:

- If using store-bought croissants, bake according to the package instructions.
- For homemade croissants, ensure they are fully baked with a golden-brown hue.

Slice and Layer:

- Allow croissants to cool slightly before slicing horizontally.
- Lay slices of prosciutto on the bottom halves of the croissants.

Arugula Topping:

- Place a handful of fresh arugula over the prosciutto.

Drizzle with Balsamic Glaze:

- Drizzle balsamic glaze over the arugula for a sweet and tangy finish.

Assemble and Serve:

- Place the top halves of the croissants on the assembled bottoms, creating a delightful combination of salty prosciutto and peppery arugula.
- Serve on a platter and enjoy the blissful flavors.

D. Caprese Croissant Bites

Ingredients:

- 6 croissants (freshly baked or store-bought)
- 150g fresh mozzarella, sliced
- 1 cup cherry tomatoes, halved
- Fresh basil leaves
- Balsamic reduction for drizzling
- Salt and pepper to taste

Instructions:

Prepare the Croissants:

- If using store-bought croissants, bake according to the package instructions.
- For homemade croissants, ensure they are fully baked with a golden-brown hue.

Slice and Arrange:

- Allow croissants to cool slightly before slicing horizontally.
- Lay slices of fresh mozzarella on the bottom halves of the croissants.

Caprese Layers:

- Add halved cherry tomatoes on top of the mozzarella.
- Place fresh basil leaves over the tomatoes.

Season and Drizzle:

- Sprinkle salt and pepper to taste.
- Drizzle balsamic reduction over the caprese layers for a burst

of flavor.

Assemble and Serve:

- Place the top halves of the croissants on the assembled bottoms, creating delightful Caprese croissant bites.
- Arrange on a platter and serve for a taste of the classic Italian combination.

E. Roasted Vegetable Medley Croissants

Ingredients:

- 6 croissants (freshly baked or store-bought)
- 1 cup assorted roasted vegetables (bell peppers, zucchini, cherry tomatoes, etc.)
- 1/2 cup herbed cream cheese
- Fresh parsley, chopped, for garnish
- Olive oil for drizzling
- Salt and pepper to taste

Instructions:
Prepare the Croissants:

- If using store-bought croissants, bake according to the package instructions.
- For homemade croissants, ensure they are fully baked with a golden-brown hue.

Slice and Spread:

- Allow croissants to cool slightly before slicing horizontally.
- Spread a layer of herbed cream cheese on the bottom halves of the croissants.

Roasted Vegetable Topping:

- Arrange assorted roasted vegetables over the cream cheese.

Drizzle and Garnish:

- Drizzle olive oil over the roasted vegetables.
- Sprinkle chopped fresh parsley for a burst of herbaceous

flavor.

Assemble and Serve:

- Place the top halves of the croissants on the assembled bottoms, creating a medley of flavors and textures.
- Serve on a platter for a vegetable-packed croissant canapé experience.

Feel free to enjoy these complementary recipes or let me know if there's anything else you'd like!

IV. Chapter 3: Innovative Croissant Canapé Creations

A. Spicy Shrimp and Avocado Fusion

Ingredients:

- 6 croissants (freshly baked or store-bought)
- 200g shrimp, peeled and deveined
- 1 tablespoon olive oil
- 1 teaspoon smoked paprika
- 1/2 teaspoon cayenne pepper (adjust to taste)
- Salt and black pepper to taste
- 2 ripe avocados, mashed
- 1 lime, juiced
- Fresh cilantro, chopped, for garnish

Instructions:

Prepare the Croissants:

- If using store-bought croissants, bake according to the package instructions.
- For homemade croissants, ensure they are fully baked with a golden-brown hue.

Spicy Shrimp:

- In a pan, heat olive oil over medium heat.
- Season shrimp with smoked paprika, cayenne pepper, salt, and black pepper.
- Cook shrimp until pink and opaque, about 2-3 minutes per side.

Avocado Mash:

- In a bowl, mash avocados and mix with lime juice.

Assemble:

- Slice the croissants horizontally.
- Spread a layer of the avocado mash on the bottom halves.
- Place a few spicy shrimp on top.
- Garnish with chopped cilantro.

Serve Fresh:

- Place the top halves of the croissants on the assembled bottoms.
- Serve immediately for a fusion of spicy shrimp and creamy avocado.

B. Cranberry and Goat Cheese Croissant Squares

Ingredients:

- 6 croissants (freshly baked or store-bought)
- 1/2 cup goat cheese, softened
- 1/4 cup dried cranberries
- 2 tablespoons honey
- Fresh rosemary, chopped, for garnish

Instructions:
Prepare the Croissants:

- If using store-bought croissants, bake according to the package instructions.
- For homemade croissants, ensure they are fully baked with a golden-brown hue.

Goat Cheese Spread:

- Allow goat cheese to soften to room temperature.
- Spread a generous layer of goat cheese on the bottom halves of the croissants.

Cranberry Topping:

- Sprinkle dried cranberries over the goat cheese.

Drizzle with Honey:

- Drizzle honey over the cranberries for a touch of sweetness.

Garnish:

- Sprinkle chopped fresh rosemary for a fragrant and herbal garnish.

Assemble and Serve:

- Place the top halves of the croissants on the assembled bottoms, creating delectable croissant squares.
- Serve on a platter for an elegant combination of creamy goat cheese, tart cranberries, and sweet honey.

C. Pesto Chicken Puff Pastry Pockets

Ingredients:

- 6 puff pastry squares (store-bought or homemade)
- 1 cup cooked chicken, shredded
- 1/4 cup pesto sauce
- 1/2 cup cherry tomatoes, halved
- 1/4 cup Parmesan cheese, grated
- Fresh basil leaves for garnish

Instructions:

Prepare the Puff Pastry:

- If using store-bought puff pastry, follow the package instructions.
- For homemade puff pastry, ensure it's fully baked and golden-brown.

Pesto Chicken Filling:

- In a bowl, mix shredded chicken with pesto sauce.

Assemble:

- Place a spoonful of the pesto chicken mixture in the center of each puff pastry square.
- Add halved cherry tomatoes on top.
- Sprinkle grated Parmesan cheese.

Fold and Seal:

- Fold the puff pastry squares diagonally, creating triangles.
- Seal the edges by pressing with a fork.

Bake:

- Bake according to the puff pastry package instructions or until golden and puffed.

Garnish and Serve:

- Garnish with fresh basil leaves.
- Serve warm for a savory and flaky puff pastry pocket.

Continue with the remaining innovative croissant canapé creations, or let me know if you'd like details on any specific one!

D. Sundried Tomato and Feta Stuffed Croissants

Ingredients:

- 6 croissants (freshly baked or store-bought)
- 1/2 cup sundried tomatoes, chopped
- 1/2 cup feta cheese, crumbled
- 2 tablespoons fresh basil, chopped
- 1 tablespoon olive oil
- Black pepper to taste

Instructions:
Prepare the Croissants:

- If using store-bought croissants, bake according to the package instructions.
- For homemade croissants, ensure they are fully baked with a golden-brown hue.

Sundried Tomato and Feta Filling:

- In a bowl, mix chopped sundried tomatoes, crumbled feta, chopped fresh basil, and olive oil.
- Season with black pepper to taste.

Slice and Stuff:

- Slice the croissants horizontally.
- Spoon the sundried tomato and feta mixture onto the bottom halves of the croissants.

Assemble and Serve:

- Place the top halves of the croissants on the assembled bottoms, creating a flavorful stuffed croissant.
- Serve on a platter for a savory blend of Mediterranean-inspired ingredients.

E. Mango Salsa Turkey Croissant Spirals

Ingredients:

- 6 croissants (freshly baked or store-bought)
- 200g cooked turkey, thinly sliced
- 1 ripe mango, diced
- 1/2 red onion, finely chopped
- 1/2 red bell pepper, diced
- 1/4 cup fresh cilantro, chopped
- Juice of 1 lime
- Salt and pepper to taste

Instructions:
Prepare the Croissants:

- If using store-bought croissants, bake according to the package instructions.
- For homemade croissants, ensure they are fully baked with a golden-brown hue.

Mango Salsa:

- In a bowl, combine diced mango, chopped red onion, diced red bell pepper, chopped cilantro, lime juice, salt, and pepper. Mix well to create a refreshing mango salsa.

Slice and Layer:

- Slice the croissants horizontally.
- Place slices of cooked turkey on the bottom halves of the croissants.

Mango Salsa Topping:

- Spoon the mango salsa over the turkey slices, ensuring a vibrant mix of colors and flavors.

Roll and Serve:

- Carefully roll each croissant from the bottom to the top, creating spiral canapés.
- Arrange on a platter and serve for a delightful combination of savory turkey and sweet mango salsa.

Enjoy these innovative croissant canapé creations, and feel free to ask if you have any more requests or questions!

V. Chapter 4: Sweet Croissant Canapés
A. Chocolate Hazelnut Croissant Bites

Ingredients:

- 6 croissants (freshly baked or store-bought)
- 1/2 cup chocolate hazelnut spread
- 1/4 cup toasted hazelnuts, chopped
- Powdered sugar for dusting

Instructions:
Prepare the Croissants:

- If using store-bought croissants, bake according to the package instructions.
- For homemade croissants, ensure they are fully baked with a golden-brown hue.

Spread Chocolate Hazelnut:

- Allow croissants to cool slightly before slicing horizontally.
- Spread a generous layer of chocolate hazelnut spread on the bottom halves of the croissants.

Chopped Hazelnut Topping:

- Sprinkle chopped toasted hazelnuts over the chocolate hazelnut spread.

Assemble and Dust:

- Place the top halves of the croissants on the assembled bottoms, creating delightful croissant bites.

- Dust with powdered sugar for an extra touch of sweetness.

B. Raspberry Almond Cream Croissant Pinwheels

Ingredients:

- 6 croissants (freshly baked or store-bought)
- 1/2 cup almond cream (almond paste mixed with cream)
- 1/2 cup fresh raspberries
- Sliced almonds for garnish
- Honey for drizzling

Instructions:
Prepare the Croissants:

- If using store-bought croissants, bake according to the package instructions.
- For homemade croissants, ensure they are fully baked with a golden-brown hue.

Almond Cream Spread:

- Allow croissants to cool slightly before slicing horizontally.
- Spread a layer of almond cream on the bottom halves of the croissants.

Fresh Raspberry Layer:

- Place fresh raspberries over the almond cream.

Roll and Slice:

- Roll each croissant from the bottom to the top to create pinwheels.
- Slice the rolled croissants into bite-sized pinwheels.

Garnish and Drizzle:

- Garnish with sliced almonds for added texture.
- Drizzle honey over the pinwheels for a touch of sweetness.

C. Lemon Curd and Blueberry Croissant Crescents

Ingredients:

- 6 croissants (freshly baked or store-bought)
- 1/2 cup lemon curd
- 1/2 cup fresh blueberries
- Powdered sugar for dusting

Instructions:
Prepare the Croissants:

- If using store-bought croissants, bake according to the package instructions.
- For homemade croissants, ensure they are fully baked with a golden-brown hue.

Lemon Curd Spread:

- Allow croissants to cool slightly before slicing horizontally.
- Spread a layer of lemon curd on the bottom halves of the croissants.

Blueberry Topping:

- Place fresh blueberries over the lemon curd.

Fold and Dust:

- Fold the top halves of the croissants over the blueberry and lemon curd layer.
- Dust with powdered sugar for a touch of sweetness.

D. Apple Cinnamon Croissant Rolls

Ingredients:

- 6 croissants (freshly baked or store-bought)
- 2 apples, peeled, cored, and thinly sliced
- 1/4 cup brown sugar
- 1 teaspoon ground cinnamon
- 2 tablespoons butter, melted
- Vanilla glaze (powdered sugar, milk, and vanilla extract)

Instructions:
Prepare the Croissants:

- If using store-bought croissants, bake according to the package instructions.
- For homemade croissants, ensure they are fully baked with a golden-brown hue.

Apple Cinnamon Filling:

- In a bowl, toss apple slices with brown sugar and ground cinnamon.

Spread and Roll:

- Allow croissants to cool slightly before slicing horizontally.
- Spread melted butter on the bottom halves and distribute the apple cinnamon mixture.

Roll and Bake:

- Roll each croissant from the bottom to the top to create rolls.
- Place the rolled croissants on a baking sheet and bake until

golden.

Vanilla Glaze:

- While the rolls are still warm, drizzle with vanilla glaze made from powdered sugar, milk, and vanilla extract.

E. Nutella and Banana Croissant Pockets

Ingredients:

- 6 croissants (freshly baked or store-bought)
- 1/2 cup Nutella
- 2 bananas, sliced
- Chopped hazelnuts for garnish

Instructions:
Prepare the Croissants:

- If using store-bought croissants, bake according to the package instructions.
- For homemade croissants, ensure they are fully baked with a golden-brown hue.

Nutella and Banana Filling:

- Allow croissants to cool slightly before slicing horizontally.
- Spread a layer of Nutella on the bottom halves of the croissants.
- Please take care of yourself

Banana Slices:

- Place banana slices over the Nutella layer.

Fold and Garnish:

- Fold the top halves of the croissants over the banana and Nutella layer.
- Garnish with chopped hazelnuts for added crunch.

Enjoy these sweet croissant canapés, and feel free to ask if you have any more requests or questions!

VI. Chapter 5: Croissant Canapé Plating and Presentation

A. Stylish Serving Suggestions

When presenting your croissant canapés, consider these stylish serving suggestions to enhance the overall dining experience:

Elevated Platters:

- Choose elegant platters or serving boards that complement the theme of your event or the style of your croissant canapés.

Mix of Shapes and Sizes:

- Create visual interest by incorporating a mix of plate shapes and sizes. This diversity adds a dynamic element to the presentation.

Tiered Displays:

- Use tiered serving stands to showcase your croissant canapés at different heights. This not only looks visually appealing but also makes it easy for guests to reach different varieties.

Decorative Linens:

- Place decorative linens or napkins under the platters to add texture and color to the presentation. Choose colors that complement the ingredients of your canapés.

Fresh Floral Arrangements:

- Incorporate small floral arrangements or edible flowers as centerpieces. This adds a touch of freshness and elegance to the display.

B. Garnishing and Decorating Techniques

Enhance the visual appeal of your croissant canapés with creative garnishing and decorating techniques:

Microgreens and Herbs:

- Garnish with microgreens or fresh herbs like parsley, basil, or chives. This not only adds a burst of color but also imparts a hint of complementary flavors.

Edible Flowers:

- Use edible flowers such as pansies, nasturtiums, or violets to add a delicate and gourmet touch to your canapés.

Citrus Zest:

- Sprinkle citrus zest (lemon, lime, or orange) over the canapés. The vibrant colors and citrus aroma enhance the overall sensory experience.

Sesame or Poppy Seeds:

- Lightly sprinkle sesame seeds or poppy seeds on top of cream cheese or other spreads for added texture and visual interest.

Balsamic Reduction Drizzle:

- Create artistic patterns by drizzling balsamic reduction over savory canapés. This adds a touch of sophistication to the presentation.

C. Creating a Croissant Canapé Platter

Assemble an enticing croissant canapé platter that captures attention and invites guests to indulge:

Organized Arrangement:

- Arrange the croissant canapés in an organized manner on the platter. Group similar flavors or types together for a cohesive look.

Variety in Heights:

- Place taller or larger canapés towards the back of the platter and shorter ones towards the front. This adds dimension and makes all the canapés visible.

Color Coordination:

- Consider color coordination when arranging canapés. This creates a visually appealing display, especially if you have a variety of colorful ingredients.

Space for Garnishes:

- Leave small spaces on the platter for additional garnishes, herbs, or edible flowers. This allows you to enhance the presentation just before serving.

Labeling Cards:

- If you have a variety of flavors, consider using small labeling cards to inform guests about each canapé. This adds a personalized touch and helps guests navigate the selection.

By incorporating these plating and presentation techniques, you'll elevate the visual appeal of your croissant canapés, making them not only delicious but also a feast for the eyes.

VII. Chapter 6: Hosting the Perfect Croissant Canapé Party

A. Planning and Preparation

Hosting a successful croissant canapé party involves careful planning and preparation to ensure a delightful experience for your guests. Consider the following steps:

Guest List and Invitations:

- Create a guest list and send out invitations well in advance. Specify the date, time, and location of the event, and request RSVPs to facilitate planning.

Menu Planning:

- Plan a diverse menu that includes a selection of savory and sweet croissant canapés. Consider dietary preferences and restrictions of your guests.

Croissant Preparation:

- Decide whether you'll be making the croissants from scratch or using store-bought ones. Plan your baking or purchasing schedule to ensure freshness.

Ingredient Shopping:

- Compile a comprehensive shopping list for all ingredients needed for your croissant canapés. Consider purchasing fresh, high-quality ingredients for the best results.

Decor and Ambiance:

- Plan the decor and ambiance of the event space. Consider a theme or color scheme that complements the style of your croissant canapés.

Seating Arrangements:

- Arrange seating to encourage socializing. Provide a mix of seating options, including comfortable chairs and standing areas for a dynamic atmosphere.

Music Selection:

- Curate a playlist or choose background music that enhances the ambiance of the party. Ensure the volume is conducive to conversation.

B. Beverage Pairing Suggestions

Offering thoughtfully paired beverages enhances the overall dining experience. Consider these beverage pairing suggestions for your croissant canapé party:

Champagne or Sparkling Wine:

- The effervescence of champagne or sparkling wine complements the flaky texture of croissants. It's a classic and celebratory choice.

White Wine:

- Choose a crisp and light white wine, such as Sauvignon Blanc or Pinot Grigio, to pair with savory croissant canapés like smoked salmon or brie and fig.

Rosé:

- A versatile rosé can pair well with a variety of both savory and sweet croissant canapés. Its acidity and fruitiness make it a crowd-pleaser.

Herbal Iced Tea:

- For a non-alcoholic option, consider serving herbal iced tea. Match flavors like mint or chamomile with your canapés for a refreshing combination.

Coffee:

- A well-brewed cup of coffee, whether black or with cream, complements sweet croissant canapés like those with chocolate or fruit fillings.

Cocktail Bar:

- Create a small cocktail bar with ingredients for a signature cocktail or a selection of classic drinks. Consider options like mimosas or bellinis for a brunch-themed event.

C. Tips for a Stress-Free Event

To ensure a stress-free croissant canapé party, keep these tips in mind:
Preparation Timeline:

- Create a timeline for the day of the event, detailing when to start baking or assembling the canapés, setting up the space, and completing any last-minute tasks.

Delegate Responsibilities:

- Enlist the help of friends or family members to assist with tasks such as serving, replenishing platters, and managing the music or beverage station.

Create a Self-Service Station:

- Arrange the croissant canapés on platters or tiered stands for easy self-service. This allows guests to mingle and serve themselves.

Temperature Considerations:

- Be mindful of the temperature of the space. If serving warm canapés, have a plan for reheating, and if serving chilled options, ensure proper refrigeration.

Relax and Enjoy:

- Remember to relax and enjoy the party. Your guests will appreciate the effort you put into hosting, and a host who is at ease sets a positive tone for the event.

By planning meticulously, pairing beverages thoughtfully, and adopting stress-free hosting strategies, you'll create a memorable croissant canapé party that your guests will cherish.

IX. Chapter 7: Global Flavors in Croissant Canapés

A. Mediterranean-Inspired Croissant Tapenade

Ingredients:

- 6 croissants (freshly baked or store-bought)
- 1 cup mixed olives (Kalamata, green, black), pitted and chopped
- 2 tablespoons capers, drained
- 2 cloves garlic, minced
- 1 tablespoon fresh parsley, chopped
- 2 tablespoons extra-virgin olive oil
- 1 teaspoon lemon zest
- Salt and black pepper to taste

Instructions:

Prepare the Croissants:

- If using store-bought croissants, bake according to the package instructions.
- For homemade croissants, ensure they are fully baked with a golden-brown hue.

Tapenade Mixture:

- In a bowl, combine chopped olives, capers, minced garlic, chopped parsley, olive oil, and lemon zest.
- Season with salt and black pepper to taste. Mix well.

Spread and Serve:

- Allow croissants to cool slightly before slicing horizontally.
- Spread a generous layer of the Mediterranean tapenade on the bottom halves of the croissants.
- Place the top halves of the croissants on the assembled bottoms, creating flavorful Mediterranean-inspired canapés.
- Serve on a platter and enjoy the bold and savory flavors.

B. Asian Fusion Crab Rangoon Croissants

Ingredients:

- 6 croissants (freshly baked or store-bought)
- 200g crab meat, cooked and shredded
- 1/2 cup cream cheese, softened
- 2 green onions, finely chopped
- 1 tablespoon soy sauce
- 1 teaspoon sesame oil
- 1/2 teaspoon garlic powder
- 1/4 teaspoon white pepper
- Sesame seeds for garnish

Instructions:
Prepare the Croissants:

- If using store-bought croissants, bake according to the package instructions.
- For homemade croissants, ensure they are fully baked with a golden-brown hue.

Crab Rangoon Filling:

- In a bowl, combine shredded crab meat, softened cream cheese, chopped green onions, soy sauce, sesame oil, garlic powder, and white pepper. Mix until well combined.

Spread and Assemble:

- Allow croissants to cool slightly before slicing horizontally.
- Spread a generous layer of the crab Rangoon mixture on the

bottom halves of the croissants.
- Place the top halves of the croissants on the assembled bottoms, creating Asian-inspired crab Rangoon canapés.
- Sprinkle sesame seeds on top for added crunch and visual appeal.

Serve Fresh:

- Arrange on a platter and serve immediately to savor the delightful fusion of flavors.

C. Latin-Influenced Chorizo and Manchego Croissant Bites

Ingredients:

- 6 croissants (freshly baked or store-bought)
- 150g chorizo, cooked and crumbled
- 1/2 cup Manchego cheese, shredded
- 1/4 cup roasted red peppers, chopped
- 2 tablespoons fresh cilantro, chopped
- 1 teaspoon smoked paprika
- Salt and black pepper to taste

Instructions:
Prepare the Croissants:

- If using store-bought croissants, bake according to the package instructions.
- For homemade croissants, ensure they are fully baked with a golden-brown hue.

Chorizo and Manchego Filling:

- In a bowl, combine crumbled chorizo, shredded Manchego cheese, chopped roasted red peppers, chopped cilantro, smoked paprika, salt, and black pepper. Mix well.

Spread and Assemble:

- Allow croissants to cool slightly before slicing horizontally.
- Spread a generous layer of the chorizo and Manchego mixture on the bottom halves of the croissants.
- Place the top halves of the croissants on the assembled

bottoms, creating Latin-inspired chorizo and Manchego canapés.

Garnish:

- Garnish with additional cilantro for a burst of freshness.

Serve on a Platter:

- Arrange on a platter and serve for a flavorful and zesty culinary experience.

Continue with the remaining global flavors in croissant canapés or let me know if you'd like details on any specific one!

D. Indian Spiced Chicken Croissant Samosas

Ingredients:

- 6 croissants (freshly baked or store-bought)
- 1 cup cooked chicken, shredded
- 1/2 cup peas, cooked
- 1/2 cup potatoes, boiled and mashed
- 1 small onion, finely chopped
- 2 cloves garlic, minced
- 1 teaspoon ginger, grated
- 1 teaspoon garam masala
- 1/2 teaspoon ground cumin
- 1/2 teaspoon ground coriander
- 1/4 teaspoon turmeric
- Salt and black pepper to taste
- Vegetable oil for frying

Instructions:
Prepare the Croissants:

- If using store-bought croissants, bake according to the package instructions.
- For homemade croissants, ensure they are fully baked with a golden-brown hue.

Samosa Filling:

- In a pan, heat a bit of vegetable oil over medium heat.
- Sauté chopped onions until translucent. Add minced garlic and grated ginger, and cook until fragrant.
- Add shredded chicken, cooked peas, mashed potatoes, garam

masala, ground cumin, ground coriander, turmeric, salt, and black pepper. Mix well and cook until the flavors meld together.

Slice and Fill:

- Allow croissants to cool slightly before slicing horizontally.
- Spoon the Indian spiced chicken mixture onto the bottom halves of the croissants.

Fold and Seal:

- Fold the croissant halves into a triangular shape, sealing the edges.

Fry or Bake:

- Either deep fry the samosas until golden brown or bake them according to the croissant package instructions until crispy.

Serve with Chutney:

- Serve the Indian spiced chicken croissant samosas with your favorite chutney for a delightful and savory experience.

E. French-Inspired Ratatouille Croissant Pockets

Ingredients:

- 6 croissants (freshly baked or store-bought)
- 1 small eggplant, diced
- 1 zucchini, diced
- 1 bell pepper (any color), diced
- 1 onion, diced
- 2 cloves garlic, minced
- 1 can (14 oz) crushed tomatoes
- 2 tablespoons tomato paste
- 1 teaspoon dried thyme
- 1 teaspoon dried rosemary
- Salt and black pepper to taste
- Olive oil for sautéing

Instructions:
repare the Croissants:

- If using store-bought croissants, bake according to the package instructions.
- For homemade croissants, ensure they are fully baked with a golden-brown hue.

Ratatouille Filling:

- In a large pan, heat olive oil over medium heat. Sauté diced eggplant, zucchini, bell pepper, onion, and minced garlic until softened.

Tomato Sauce:

- Add crushed tomatoes, tomato paste, dried thyme, dried rosemary, salt, and black pepper to the sautéed vegetables. Simmer until the sauce thickens and flavors meld.

Slice and Fill:

- Allow croissants to cool slightly before slicing horizontally.
- Spoon the ratatouille mixture onto the bottom halves of the croissants.

Fold and Serve:

- Fold the croissant halves to create pockets, enclosing the flavorful ratatouille filling.

Garnish:

- Garnish with additional fresh herbs for a touch of brightness.

Serve Warm:

- Serve the French-inspired ratatouille croissant pockets warm for a taste of classic French cuisine with a twist.

Enjoy these global flavors in croissant canapés, and let me know if you have any more requests or questions!

X. Chapter 8: Vegetarian and Vegan Croissant Canapés

A. Spinach and Artichoke Croissant Swirls

Ingredients:

- 6 croissants (freshly baked or store-bought)
- 1 cup frozen spinach, thawed and drained
- 1 cup artichoke hearts, chopped
- 1/2 cup cream cheese
- 1/2 cup grated Parmesan cheese
- 1/4 cup mayonnaise
- 2 cloves garlic, minced
- Salt and black pepper to taste

Instructions:

Prepare the Croissants:

- If using store-bought croissants, bake according to the package instructions.
- For homemade croissants, ensure they are fully baked with a golden-brown hue.

Spinach and Artichoke Filling:

- In a bowl, mix thawed and drained spinach, chopped artichoke hearts, cream cheese, grated Parmesan, mayonnaise, minced garlic, salt, and black pepper. Ensure the mixture is well combined.

Spread and Roll:

- Allow croissants to cool slightly before slicing horizontally.
- Spread the spinach and artichoke mixture onto the bottom halves of the croissants.
- Roll the croissants from the bottom to the top to create swirls.

Slice and Serve:

- Slice the rolled croissants into bite-sized pieces.
- Arrange on a platter and serve for a delectable vegetarian canapé.

B. Vegan Cream Cheese and Dill Croissant Squares

Ingredients:

- 6 croissants (freshly baked or store-bought)
- 1 cup vegan cream cheese
- 2 tablespoons fresh dill, chopped
- 1 tablespoon lemon juice
- Salt and black pepper to taste

Instructions:
Prepare the Croissants:

- If using store-bought croissants, bake according to the package instructions.
- For homemade croissants, ensure they are fully baked with a golden-brown hue.

Vegan Cream Cheese Mixture:

- In a bowl, combine vegan cream cheese, chopped fresh dill, lemon juice, salt, and black pepper. Mix well until the ingredients are evenly distributed.

Spread and Slice:

- Allow croissants to cool slightly before slicing horizontally.
- Spread a generous layer of the vegan cream cheese mixture onto the bottom halves of the croissants.

Cut into Squares:

- Cut the croissants into squares or rectangles for easy serving.

Garnish:

- Garnish with additional fresh dill for a burst of flavor.

Serve Chilled:

- Refrigerate briefly to allow the vegan cream cheese to set, then serve these refreshing croissant squares.

C. Roasted Red Pepper and Hummus Croissant Spirals

Ingredients:

- 6 croissants (freshly baked or store-bought)
- 1 cup roasted red peppers, chopped
- 1 cup hummus (store-bought or homemade)
- 2 tablespoons fresh parsley, chopped
- 1 tablespoon lemon juice
- Salt and black pepper to taste

Instructions:
Prepare the Croissants:

- If using store-bought croissants, bake according to the package instructions.
- For homemade croissants, ensure they are fully baked with a golden-brown hue.

Roasted Red Pepper and Hummus Spread:

- In a blender or food processor, combine chopped roasted red peppers, hummus, chopped fresh parsley, lemon juice, salt, and black pepper. Blend until you have a smooth and creamy spread.

Spread and Roll:

- Allow croissants to cool slightly before slicing horizontally.
- Spread a generous layer of the roasted red pepper and hummus mixture onto the bottom halves of the croissants.
- Roll the croissants from the bottom to the top to create spirals.

Slice and Serve:

- Slice the rolled croissants into bite-sized spirals.
- Arrange on a platter and serve for a delightful vegan canapé experience.

Continue with the remaining vegetarian and vegan croissant canapés, or let me know if you have any specific preferences or modifications!

D. Mushroom and Truffle Oil Croissant Crescents

Ingredients:

- 6 croissants (freshly baked or store-bought)
- 2 cups mushrooms (cremini or button), finely chopped
- 2 tablespoons truffle oil
- 1/2 cup vegan mozzarella cheese, shredded
- 2 cloves garlic, minced
- 2 tablespoons fresh chives, chopped
- Salt and black pepper to taste

Instructions:

Prepare the Croissants:

- If using store-bought croissants, bake according to the package instructions.
- For homemade croissants, ensure they are fully baked with a golden-brown hue.

Mushroom and Truffle Oil Filling:

- In a pan, sauté finely chopped mushrooms in truffle oil until they release their moisture and become golden brown.

Garlic and Cheese Addition:

- Add minced garlic to the sautéed mushrooms and cook until fragrant.
- Remove from heat and let it cool slightly before stirring in vegan mozzarella cheese and chopped fresh chives. Season with salt and black pepper.

Spread and Roll:

- Allow croissants to cool slightly before slicing horizontally.
- Spread the mushroom and truffle oil mixture onto the bottom halves of the croissants.
- Roll the croissants from the bottom to the top to create crescents.

Slice and Serve:

- Slice the rolled croissants into crescents.
- Arrange on a platter and serve these savory and aromatic croissant canapés.

E. Zucchini and Sun-Dried Tomato Croissant Pinwheels

Ingredients:

- 6 croissants (freshly baked or store-bought)
- 1 large zucchini, thinly sliced
- 1/2 cup sun-dried tomatoes, chopped
- 1/2 cup vegan feta cheese, crumbled
- 2 tablespoons fresh basil, chopped
- 2 tablespoons balsamic glaze
- Salt and black pepper to taste

Instructions:

Prepare the Croissants:

- If using store-bought croissants, bake according to the package instructions.
- For homemade croissants, ensure they are fully baked with a

Zucchini and Sun-Dried Tomato Filling:

- In a bowl, toss thinly sliced zucchini, chopped sun-dried tomatoes, crumbled vegan feta cheese, chopped fresh basil, balsamic glaze, salt, and black pepper. Ensure the ingredients are well combined.

Spread and Roll:

- Allow croissants to cool slightly before slicing horizontally.
- Spread the zucchini and sun-dried tomato mixture onto the bottom halves of the croissants.

- Roll the croissants from the bottom to the top to create pinwheels.

Slice and Serve:

- Slice the rolled croissants into bite-sized pinwheels.
- Arrange on a platter and serve these delightful and refreshing croissant pinwheels.

Enjoy these vegetarian and vegan croissant canapés, and feel free to let me know if you have any more requests or questions!

XI. Chapter 9: Breakfast-Inspired Croissant Canapés

A. Bacon, Egg, and Cheese Croissant Sliders

Ingredients:

- 6 croissants (freshly baked or store-bought)
- 6 eggs, scrambled
- 6 slices bacon, cooked
- 1 cup cheddar cheese, shredded
- Salt and black pepper to taste
- Fresh chives for garnish

Instructions:

Prepare the Croissants:

- If using store-bought croissants, bake according to the package instructions.
- For homemade croissants, ensure they are fully baked with a golden-brown hue.

Scrambled Eggs:

- In a pan, scramble the eggs until just set. Season with salt and black pepper.

Assemble Sliders:

- Allow croissants to cool slightly before slicing horizontally.
- Place a portion of scrambled eggs on the bottom halves of the croissants.

- Add a slice of cooked bacon and a sprinkle of shredded cheddar cheese.
- Place the top halves of the croissants on the assembled bottoms to create delicious breakfast sliders.

Garnish:

- **Garnish with fresh chives for a pop of color and added flavor.**

Serve Warm:

- Arrange on a platter and serve warm for a hearty breakfast canapé.

B. Sausage and Maple Syrup Croissant Breakfast Bites

Ingredients:

- 6 croissants (freshly baked or store-bought)
- 1/2 lb breakfast sausage, cooked and crumbled
- 1/4 cup maple syrup
- 1 cup cream cheese, softened
- 2 tablespoons chives, chopped
- Salt and black pepper to taste

Instructions:
Prepare the Croissants:

- If using store-bought croissants, bake according to the package instructions.
- For homemade croissants, ensure they are fully baked with a golden-brown hue.

Sausage and Maple Syrup Mixture:

- In a bowl, combine cooked and crumbled breakfast sausage, maple syrup, softened cream cheese, chopped chives, salt, and black pepper. Mix until well combined.

Spread and Slice:

- Allow croissants to cool slightly before slicing horizontally.
- Spread a generous layer of the sausage and maple syrup mixture onto the bottom halves of the croissants.

Cut into Bites:

- Cut the croissants into bite-sized pieces for easy serving.

Serve at Room Temperature:

- Allow the croissant breakfast bites to come to room temperature before serving, highlighting the savory-sweet combination.

C. Spinach and Feta Croissant Quiche Squares

Ingredients:

- 6 croissants (freshly baked or store-bought)
- 1 cup frozen spinach, thawed and drained
- 1/2 cup feta cheese, crumbled
- 1/2 cup cherry tomatoes, halved
- 4 large eggs
- 1 cup milk
- Salt and black pepper to taste
- Fresh basil for garnish

Instructions:
Prepare the Croissants:

- If using store-bought croissants, bake according to the package instructions.
- For homemade croissants, ensure they are fully baked with a golden-brown hue.

Quiche Filling:

- In a bowl, combine thawed and drained spinach, crumbled feta cheese, and halved cherry tomatoes.

Egg Mixture:

- In another bowl, whisk together eggs, milk, salt, and black pepper until well combined.

Assemble and Bake:

- Allow croissants to cool slightly before slicing horizontally.
- Place the bottom halves of the croissants in a baking dish.
- Spread the spinach and feta mixture evenly over the croissants.
- Pour the egg mixture over the top.
- Bake in the oven until the eggs are set and the top is golden brown.

Garnish:

- Garnish with fresh basil for a burst of flavor.

Slice and Serve:

- Cut the baked croissants into squares and serve these spinach and feta croissant quiche squares.

Continue with the remaining breakfast-inspired croissant canapés, or let me know if you have any specific preferences or modifications!

D. Blueberry Cream Cheese Croissant Muffins

Ingredients:

- 6 croissants (freshly baked or store-bought)
- 1 cup blueberries
- 1/2 cup cream cheese, softened
- 1/4 cup granulated sugar
- 1 teaspoon vanilla extract
- 1 large egg
- Powdered sugar for dusting (optional)

Instructions:
Prepare the Croissants:

- If using store-bought croissants, bake according to the package instructions.
- For homemade croissants, ensure they are fully baked with a golden-brown hue.

Blueberry Cream Cheese Filling:

- In a bowl, mix together softened cream cheese, granulated sugar, vanilla extract, and the egg until smooth.

Assemble Muffins:

- Allow croissants to cool slightly before slicing horizontally.
- Spread a layer of the blueberry cream cheese mixture onto the bottom halves of the croissants.
- Sprinkle blueberries over the cream cheese layer.

Top and Bake:

- Place the top halves of the croissants on the assembled bottoms to create muffin-like structures.
- Bake in the oven until the cream cheese is set and the blueberries are juicy.

Dust with Powdered Sugar:

- Optionally, dust the baked muffins with powdered sugar for a touch of sweetness and elegance.

Serve Warm:

- Arrange on a platter and serve these delightful blueberry cream cheese croissant muffins warm.

E. Hash Brown and Cheddar Croissant Pockets

Ingredients:

- 6 croissants (freshly baked or store-bought)
- 2 cups hash browns, cooked according to package instructions
- 1 cup cheddar cheese, shredded
- 1/4 cup green onions, chopped
- 1/2 cup sour cream
- Salt and black pepper to taste

Instructions:

Prepare the Croissants:

- If using store-bought croissants, bake according to the package instructions.
- For homemade croissants, ensure they are fully baked with a golden-brown hue.

Hash Brown and Cheddar Filling:

- In a bowl, combine cooked hash browns, shredded cheddar cheese, chopped green onions, sour cream, salt, and black pepper. Mix until well combined.

Spread and Fold:

- Allow croissants to cool slightly before slicing horizontally.
- Spread a generous layer of the hash brown and cheddar mixture onto the bottom halves of the croissants.

- Fold the croissants over the filling to create pockets.

Serve Warm:

- Arrange on a platter and serve these hash brown and cheddar croissant pockets warm for a savory and satisfying breakfast canapé.

Enjoy these delicious breakfast-inspired croissant canapés! If you have any more requests or questions, feel free to let me know.

XII. Chapter 10: Health-Conscious Croissant Canapés

A. Grilled Chicken and Avocado Croissant Wraps

Ingredients:

- 6 croissants (freshly baked or store-bought)
- 1 lb grilled chicken breast, sliced
- 2 avocados, thinly sliced
- 1 cup mixed greens
- 1/4 cup Greek yogurt
- 2 tablespoons lime juice
- Salt and black pepper to taste

Instructions:
Prepare the Croissants:

- If using store-bought croissants, bake according to the package instructions.
- For homemade croissants, ensure they are fully baked with a golden-brown hue.

Grilled Chicken and Avocado Filling:

- In a bowl, combine sliced grilled chicken, thinly sliced avocados, mixed greens, Greek yogurt, lime juice, salt, and black pepper. Toss until well combined.

Assemble and Wrap:

- Allow croissants to cool slightly before slicing horizontally.

- Place a generous amount of the chicken and avocado mixture on the bottom halves of the croissants.
- Wrap the croissants around the filling, creating wraps.

Slice and Serve:

- Slice the wrapped croissants diagonally for easy serving.
- Serve these grilled chicken and avocado croissant wraps for a wholesome and satisfying canapé.

B. Greek Yogurt and Berry Croissant Parfaits

Ingredients:

- 6 croissants (freshly baked or store-bought)
- 1 cup Greek yogurt
- 1 cup mixed berries (strawberries, blueberries, raspberries)
- 2 tablespoons honey
- Granola for topping (optional)

Instructions:
Prepare the Croissants:

- If using store-bought croissants, bake according to the package instructions.
- For homemade croissants, ensure they are fully baked with a golden-brown hue.

Greek Yogurt and Berry Parfait:

- In individual serving glasses or bowls, layer Greek yogurt, mixed berries, and a drizzle of honey.
- Repeat the layers until the glasses are filled.

Slice and Top:

- Allow croissants to cool slightly before slicing horizontally.
- Serve the Greek yogurt and berry parfaits on the sliced croissant halves.
- Optionally, top with granola for added crunch.

Serve Chilled:

- Refrigerate briefly before serving these refreshing and health-conscious croissant parfaits.

C. Quinoa and Vegetable-Stuffed Croissants

Ingredients:

- 6 croissants (freshly baked or store-bought)
- 1 cup cooked quinoa
- 1 cup mixed vegetables (bell peppers, cherry tomatoes, cucumbers), diced
- 1/4 cup feta cheese, crumbled
- 2 tablespoons balsamic vinaigrette
- Fresh basil for garnish

Instructions:
Prepare the Croissants:

- If using store-bought croissants, bake according to the package instructions.
- For homemade croissants, ensure they are fully baked with a golden-brown hue.

Quinoa and Vegetable Filling:

- In a bowl, combine cooked quinoa, diced mixed vegetables, crumbled feta cheese, and balsamic vinaigrette. Mix well.

Stuff the Croissants:

- Allow croissants to cool slightly before slicing horizontally.
- Fill the bottom halves of the croissants with the quinoa and vegetable mixture.

Garnish:

- Garnish with fresh basil for a burst of flavor and added freshness.

Serve Open-Faced:

- Serve these quinoa and vegetable-stuffed croissants open-faced for a light and nutritious canapé.

Continue with the remaining health-conscious croissant canapés, or let me know if you have any specific preferences or modifications!

D. Turkey and Cranberry Croissant Lettuce Wraps

Ingredients:

- 6 croissants (freshly baked or store-bought)
- 1 lb turkey breast, thinly sliced
- 1/2 cup cranberry sauce
- 1 cup mixed salad greens
- 1/4 cup almonds, sliced
- 2 tablespoons Dijon mustard
- Salt and black pepper to taste

Instructions:
Prepare the Croissants:

- If using store-bought croissants, bake according to the package instructions.
- For homemade croissants, ensure they are fully baked with a golden-brown hue.

Turkey and Cranberry Filling:

- In a bowl, combine thinly sliced turkey breast, cranberry sauce, mixed salad greens, sliced almonds, Dijon mustard, salt, and black pepper. Toss until well combined.

Assemble and Wrap:

- Allow croissants to cool slightly before slicing horizontally.
- Place a generous amount of the turkey and cranberry mixture on the bottom halves of the croissants.
- Wrap the croissants around the filling, creating lettuce wraps.

Slice and Serve:

- Slice the wrapped croissants diagonally for easy serving.
- Serve these turkey and cranberry croissant lettuce wraps for a delightful and wholesome canapé.

E. Smashed Chickpea and Cucumber Croissant Rounds

Ingredients:

- 6 croissants (freshly baked or store-bought)
- 1 can (15 oz) chickpeas, drained and rinsed
- 1 cucumber, finely diced
- 1/4 cup red onion, finely chopped
- 2 tablespoons lemon juice
- 1/4 cup fresh cilantro, chopped
- 2 tablespoons olive oil
- Salt and black pepper to taste

Instructions:
Prepare the Croissants:

- If using store-bought croissants, bake according to the package instructions.
- For homemade croissants, ensure they are fully baked with a golden-brown hue.

Smashed Chickpea and Cucumber Filling:

- In a bowl, smash the chickpeas with a fork or potato masher.
- Add finely diced cucumber, chopped red onion, lemon juice, chopped fresh cilantro, olive oil, salt, and black pepper. Mix until well combined.

Spread on Croissant Rounds:

- Allow croissants to cool slightly before slicing horizontally.
- Spread a generous layer of the smashed chickpea and

cucumber mixture onto the croissant rounds.

Garnish:

- Garnish with additional cilantro for a fresh and vibrant touch.

Serve Open-Faced:

- Serve these smashed chickpea and cucumber croissant rounds open-faced for a light and flavorful canapé experience.

Enjoy these health-conscious croissant canapés! If you have any more requests or questions, feel free to let me know.

XIII. Chapter 11: Mini Croissant Desserts

A. Miniature Croissant Fruit Tarts

Ingredients:

- 6 mini croissants (freshly baked or store-bought)
- 1 cup vanilla pastry cream
- Assorted fresh fruits (berries, kiwi, mango), sliced
- Apricot glaze (apricot jam mixed with water)
- Fresh mint leaves for garnish

Instructions:
Prepare the Mini Croissants:

- If using store-bought mini croissants, bake according to the package instructions.
- For homemade mini croissants, ensure they are fully baked with a golden-brown hue.

Assemble Fruit Tarts:

- Slice the mini croissants horizontally.
- Spread a layer of vanilla pastry cream on the bottom halves of the croissants.
- Arrange sliced fresh fruits on top of the pastry cream.

Apricot Glaze:

- Heat apricot jam with a splash of water until it becomes a glaze.
- Brush the glaze over the fresh fruits for a glossy finish.

Garnish:

- Garnish each mini croissant fruit tart with fresh mint leaves.

Serve Chilled:

- Chill the mini croissant fruit tarts before serving for a refreshing dessert bite.

B. Petite Pistachio and Raspberry Croissant Napoleons

Ingredients:

- 6 mini croissants (freshly baked or store-bought)
- 1 cup pistachio cream (pistachio paste mixed with whipped cream)
- Fresh raspberries
- Powdered sugar for dusting
- Crushed pistachios for garnish

Instructions:

Prepare the Mini Croissants:

- If using store-bought mini croissants, bake according to the package instructions.
- For homemade mini croissants, ensure they are fully baked with a golden-brown hue.

Pistachio Cream Filling:

- In a bowl, mix pistachio paste with whipped cream to create a pistachio cream.

Assemble Croissant Napoleons:

- Slice the mini croissants horizontally.
- Spread a generous layer of pistachio cream on the bottom halves of the croissants.
- Place fresh raspberries on top of the cream.

Stack and Dust:

- Stack another croissant half on top to create a petite croissant napoleon.
- Dust with powdered sugar and garnish with crushed pistachios.

Serve Individually:

- Serve these petite pistachio and raspberry croissant napoleons as delightful individual desserts.

C. Tiny Tiramisu Croissant Cups

Ingredients:

- 6 mini croissants (freshly baked or store-bought)
- 1 cup espresso, cooled
- 1/2 cup mascarpone cheese
- 1/4 cup sugar
- 1 teaspoon vanilla extract
- Cocoa powder for dusting

Instructions:
Prepare the Mini Croissants:

- If using store-bought mini croissants, bake according to the package instructions.
- For homemade mini croissants, ensure they are fully baked with a golden-brown hue.

Tiramisu Filling:

- In a bowl, whisk together mascarpone cheese, sugar, and vanilla extract until smooth.

Assemble Croissant Cups:

- Slice the mini croissants horizontally.
- Dip the croissant halves into cooled espresso, ensuring they are moistened but not overly soaked.
- Spread a layer of tiramisu filling on the bottom halves of the croissants.

Stack and Dust:

- Stack another croissant half on top to create a tiny tiramisu croissant cup.
- Dust with cocoa powder for the classic tiramisu finish.

Serve Chilled:

- Chill the tiny tiramisu croissant cups before serving for a delightful and indulgent dessert.

D. Chocolate-Dipped Croissant Strawberries

Ingredients:

- 6 mini croissants (freshly baked or store-bought)
- 1 cup chocolate chips (dark or milk chocolate)
- Fresh strawberries, washed and dried

Instructions:
Prepare the Mini Croissants:

- If using store-bought mini croissants, bake according to the package instructions.
- For homemade mini croissants, ensure they are fully baked with a golden-brown hue.

Melt Chocolate:

- Melt chocolate chips in a heatproof bowl using a double boiler or in short intervals in the microwave, stirring until smooth.

Dip Croissant Strawberries:

- Dip each strawberry into the melted chocolate, ensuring they are well-coated.
- Place the chocolate-dipped strawberries on the bottom halves of the sliced croissants.

Set and Serve:

- Allow the chocolate to set before serving these delectable chocolate-dipped croissant strawberries.

E. Espresso-Infused Croissant Affogato Bites

Ingredients:

- 6 mini croissants (freshly baked or store-bought)
- Vanilla ice cream
- Espresso or strong brewed coffee
- Chocolate shavings for garnish

Instructions:
Prepare the Mini Croissants:

- If using store-bought mini croissants, bake according to the package instructions.
- For homemade mini croissants, ensure they are fully baked with a golden-brown hue.

Assemble Croissant Affogato Bites:

- Slice the mini croissants horizontally.
- Place a small scoop of vanilla ice cream on the bottom halves of the croissants.

Pour Espresso:

- Pour a shot of hot espresso or strong brewed coffee over the vanilla ice cream.

Garnish:

- Garnish with chocolate shavings for an extra layer of indulgence.

Serve Immediately:

- Serve these espresso-infused croissant affogato bites immediately for a delightful and caffeinated dessert experience.

Indulge in the sweetness of these mini croissant desserts, and feel free to let me know if you have any more requests or questions!

XIV. Chapter 12: Croissant Canapé Dips and Spreads

A. Sundried Tomato and Basil Croissant Dip

Ingredients:

- 6 croissants (freshly baked or store-bought)
- 1/2 cup sundried tomatoes, packed in oil, drained
- 1/4 cup fresh basil leaves
- 1/2 cup cream cheese
- 1 clove garlic, minced
- Salt and black pepper to taste

Instructions:
Prepare the Croissants:

- If using store-bought croissants, bake according to the package instructions.
- For homemade croissants, ensure they are fully baked with a golden-brown hue.

Sundried Tomato and Basil Dip:

- In a food processor, combine sundried tomatoes, fresh basil, cream cheese, minced garlic, salt, and black pepper.
- Blend until smooth and well combined.

Chill and Serve:

- Chill the sundried tomato and basil croissant dip before serving for enhanced flavor.

- Serve with sliced croissants for a delightful dipping experience.

B. Whipped Feta and Olive Croissant Spread

Ingredients:

- 6 croissants (freshly baked or store-bought)
- 1 cup feta cheese, crumbled
- 1/4 cup Kalamata olives, pitted and chopped
- 2 tablespoons olive oil
- 1 teaspoon lemon zest
- Fresh thyme for garnish

Instructions:
Prepare the Croissants:

- If using store-bought croissants, bake according to the package instructions.
- For homemade croissants, ensure they are fully baked with a golden-brown hue.

Whipped Feta and Olive Spread:

- In a food processor, combine crumbled feta cheese, chopped Kalamata olives, olive oil, and lemon zest.
- Blend until the mixture becomes a smooth and whipped spread.

Garnish and Serve:

- Transfer the whipped feta and olive croissant spread to a serving bowl.
- Garnish with fresh thyme.
- Serve with sliced croissants for a Mediterranean-inspired

treat.

C. Honey Mustard Dipping Sauce for Croissant Nuggets

Ingredients:

- 6 croissants (freshly baked or store-bought), cut into nugget-sized pieces
- 1/4 cup Dijon mustard
- 2 tablespoons honey
- 1 tablespoon mayonnaise
- 1 teaspoon lemon juice
- Pinch of cayenne pepper (optional)

Instructions:
Prepare the Croissants:

- If using store-bought croissants, bake according to the package instructions.
- For homemade croissants, ensure they are fully baked with a golden-brown hue.
- Cut into nugget-sized pieces.

Honey Mustard Dipping Sauce:

- In a bowl, whisk together Dijon mustard, honey, mayonnaise, lemon juice, and cayenne pepper (if using).
- Adjust the sweetness and spiciness to taste.

Serve Warm:

- Warm the honey mustard dipping sauce slightly before serving.
- Arrange the croissant nuggets on a platter with the dipping

sauce on the side for a delightful snack.

D. Guacamole and Salsa Croissant Scoops

Ingredients:

- 6 croissants (freshly baked or store-bought)
- 1 cup guacamole
- 1 cup salsa (homemade or store-bought)
- Fresh cilantro for garnish

Instructions:
Prepare the Croissants:

- If using store-bought croissants, bake according to the package instructions.
- For homemade croissants, ensure they are fully baked with a golden-brown hue.

Assemble Croissant Scoops:

- Slice the croissants horizontally and then cut each half into smaller, bite-sized pieces.
- Spoon a dollop of guacamole onto each croissant piece.
- Top with salsa.

Garnish and Serve:

- Garnish with fresh cilantro.
- Serve these guacamole and salsa croissant scoops as a crowd-pleasing appetizer.

E. Roasted Red Pepper Hummus Croissant Dunkers

Ingredients:

- 6 croissants (freshly baked or store-bought)
- 1 cup roasted red pepper hummus
- 1/4 cup pine nuts, toasted
- Fresh parsley for garnish

Instructions:
Prepare the Croissants:

- If using store-bought croissants, bake according to the package instructions.
- For homemade croissants, ensure they are fully baked with a golden-brown hue.

Assemble Croissant Dunkers:

- Slice the croissants horizontally.
- Spread a layer of roasted red pepper hummus on the bottom halves of the croissants.

Sprinkle and Garnish:

- Sprinkle toasted pine nuts over the hummus layer.
- Garnish with fresh parsley.

Serve and Dunk:

- Serve these roasted red pepper hummus croissant dunkers for a flavorful and satisfying dipping experience.

Enjoy these delectable croissant canapé dips and spreads! If you have any more requests or questions, feel free to let me know.

VIII. Conclusion
A. Recap of Key Tips and Techniques

In this culinary journey through the art of croissant canapés, we've explored various techniques to elevate your creations. Here's a recap of key tips and techniques:

Selecting the Perfect Croissants:

- Choose high-quality croissants, whether homemade or store-bought, for the foundation of your canapés.

Proper Slicing and Shaping:

- Master the art of slicing croissants horizontally for optimal presentation and ease of assembly.

Baking Tips for Flaky Perfection:

- Follow baking instructions meticulously to achieve a golden-brown, flaky texture that defines a perfect croissant.

Storing and Reheating Croissants:

- Learn effective methods for storing and reheating croissants to maintain their freshness and texture.

Flavor Combinations:

- Explore a diverse range of flavor combinations, from classic to innovative, to delight your taste buds and those of your guests.

Presentation and Plating:

- Elevate the visual appeal of your croissant canapés through stylish serving suggestions, garnishing techniques, and creating eye-catching platters.

B. Encouragement to Experiment with Flavors

The world of croissant canapés is vast and open to experimentation. Don't be afraid to infuse your personal style and culinary preferences into these delightful creations. Experiment with unexpected flavor pairings, unique fillings, and inventive presentations. Your imagination is the limit, and each experiment is an opportunity to craft something extraordinary.

C. Final Thoughts on the Art of Croissant Canapés

As you embark on your croissant canapé adventures, remember that the art lies not just in the flavors but also in the joy of crafting something beautiful and delicious. Whether you're hosting a gathering, treating yourself, or surprising loved ones, the process of creating and sharing croissant canapés is a celebration of creativity and the pleasure of good food.

May your croissant canapés be a testament to your passion for the culinary arts, leaving a lasting impression on every palate they grace. Bon appétit!

www.ingramcontent.com/pod-product-compliance
Lightning Source LLC
Chambersburg PA
CBHW022157150726
47992CB00002B/836